W9-BFM-112

Celtic Borders & Decoration

Celtic Borders & Decoration

Courtney Davis

Text by Helena Paterson

CASSELL&CO

First published in the UK 1992 by Blandford
Cassell & Co.
Orion House
5 Upper Saint Martin's Lane
London WC2H 9EA

Reprinted 1993 (twice), 1994, 1995, 1996 (twice),
1997, 1998, 1999 (twice), 2001

Copyright © 1992 Courtney Davis
Text copyright © 1992 Helena Paterson

All rights reserved. No part of this book
may be reproduced or transmitted
in any form or by any means,
electronic or mechanical, including photocopying,
recording or any information storage
and retrieval system, without prior permission
in writing from the copyright holder and Publisher.

Distributed in the United States
by Sterling Publishing Co., Inc.
387 Park Avenue South, New York, NY 10016–8810

Cataloguing in Publication Data
for this title is available at the British Library

ISBN 0-7137-2330-0

Typeset by Litho Link Ltd., Welshpool, Powys
Printed and bound in Great Britain by
Latimer Trend & Company Ltd., Plymouth

contents

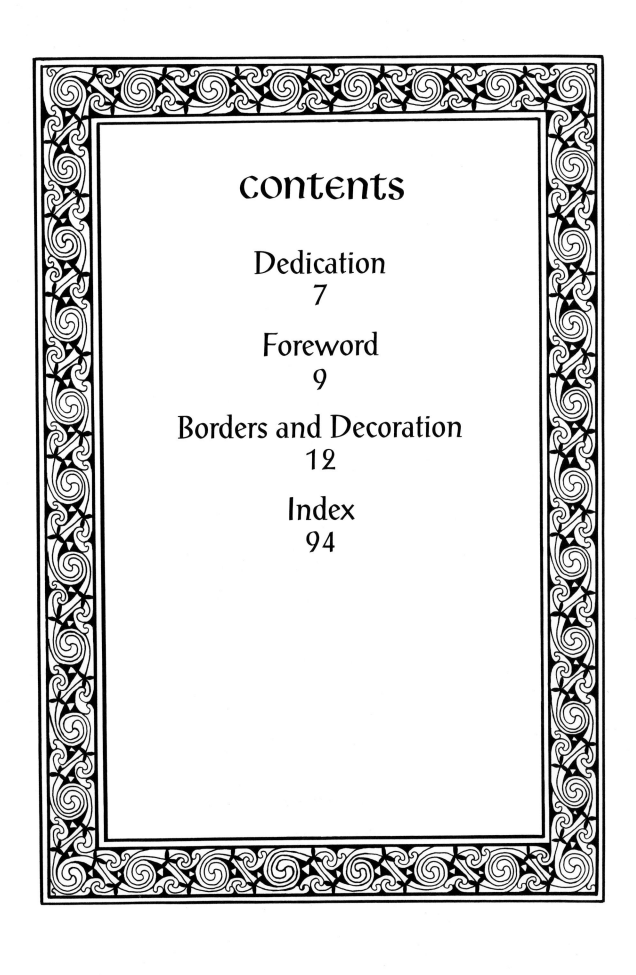

Dedicated
to Dimity
&
The Merlin
Energy

Courtney Davis is the author and
illustrator of
THE CELTIC ART SOURCE BOOK
Published by Blandford

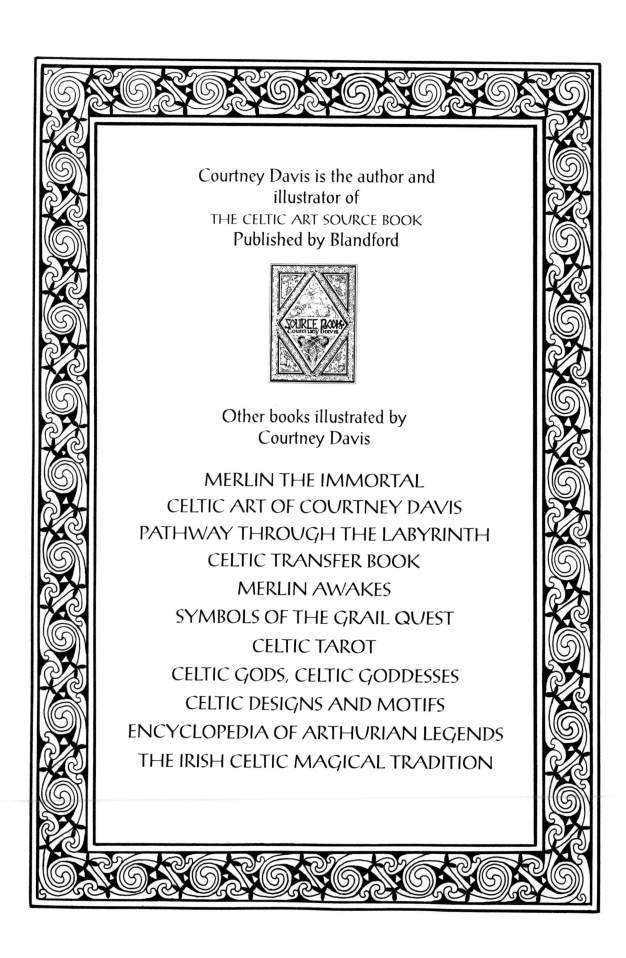

Other books illustrated by
Courtney Davis

MERLIN THE IMMORTAL
CELTIC ART OF COURTNEY DAVIS
PATHWAY THROUGH THE LABYRINTH
CELTIC TRANSFER BOOK
MERLIN AWAKES
SYMBOLS OF THE GRAIL QUEST
CELTIC TAROT
CELTIC GODS, CELTIC GODDESSES
CELTIC DESIGNS AND MOTIFS
ENCYCLOPEDIA OF ARTHURIAN LEGENDS
THE IRISH CELTIC MAGICAL TRADITION

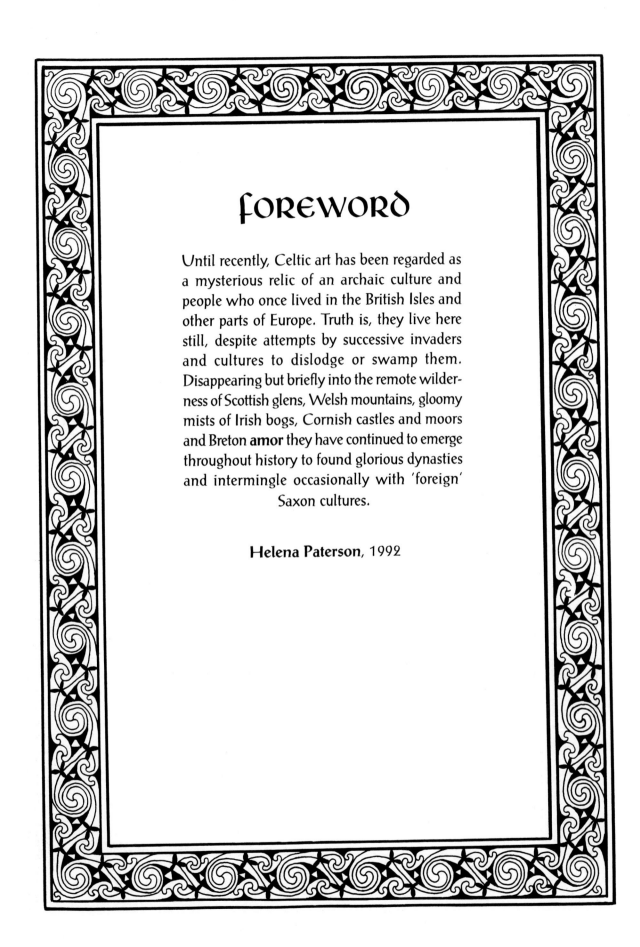

foREWORD

Until recently, Celtic art has been regarded as
a mysterious relic of an archaic culture and
people who once lived in the British Isles and
other parts of Europe. Truth is, they live here
still, despite attempts by successive invaders
and cultures to dislodge or swamp them.
Disappearing but briefly into the remote wilder-
ness of Scottish glens, Welsh mountains, gloomy
mists of Irish bogs, Cornish castles and moors
and Breton **amor** they have continued to emerge
throughout history to found glorious dynasties
and intermingle occasionally with 'foreign'
Saxon cultures.

Helena Paterson, 1992

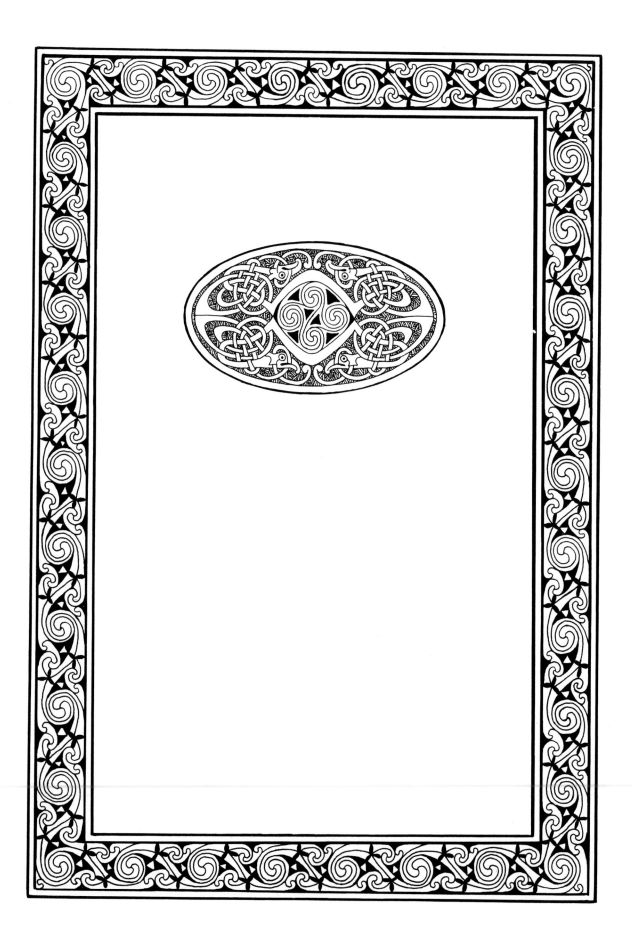

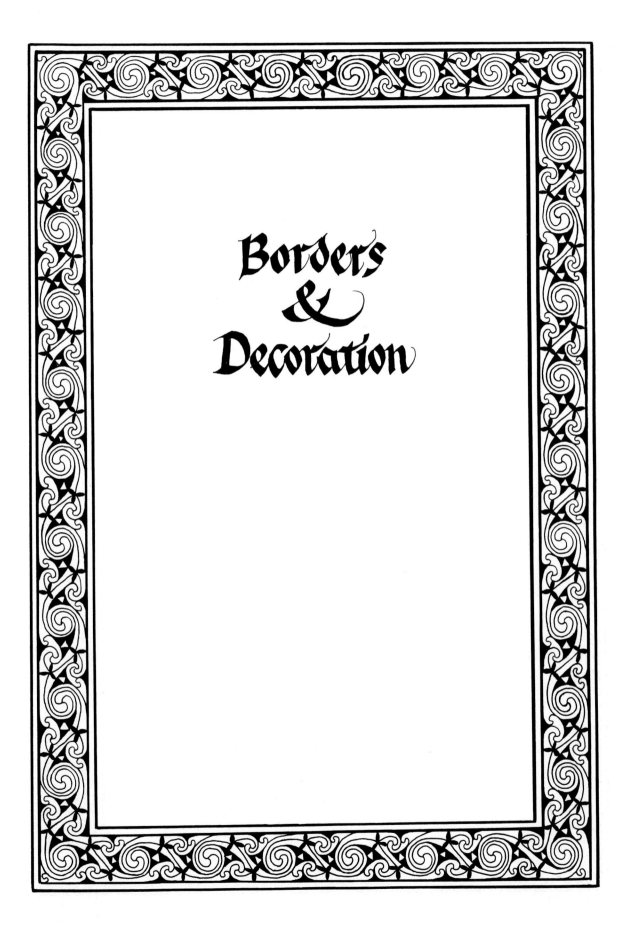

Borders
&
Decoration

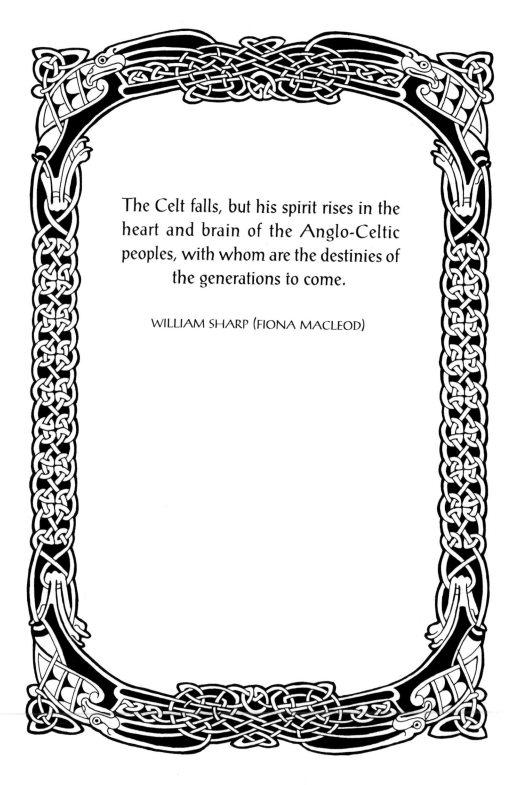

The Celt falls, but his spirit rises in the heart and brain of the Anglo-Celtic peoples, with whom are the destinies of the generations to come.

WILLIAM SHARP (FIONA MACLEOD)

'Birds of Friendship': Originally designed in 1987 for the back of a series of greeting cards published by New World Cassettes.

bar

13

'Challenge' (1984) Illustration taken from
Merlin the Immortal written by Peter Quiller.

Fabric designs (1991) adapted from the
Lindisfarne Gospels.

Fabric design (1992) adapted from the
Lindisfarne Gospels.

Key pattern carpet design (1992).

The Celtic artists left a legacy of a classical style that subscribes to a classical culture and people. They were not the barbarians referred to by the invading Romans — whose own history is less than humane, despite their illustrious trappings of civilization. Perhaps the Irish have the most authentic records concerning the origins of their race, and their most famous manuscript **The Book of Kells** in the Library of Trinity College, Dublin, is the most magnificent example of Celtic Art. To appreciate fully this unique art form is to know something of their culture and origins. Irish scholars identify the Celts, who were known as the Milesians, as a mediterranean Bronze–Age people coming originally from the Minoan–Crete (Mycenean) civilization of ancient Greece. To many, the spiral symbols found at the New Grange passage-grave in Ireland confirms the Mycenean link, and is perhaps the spiritual source of Celtic Art.

However, the Celts did not build the New Grange nor any of the Megalithic stone monuments found in Britain and Ireland. According to the Irish, the people who built New Grange were the first proto-Celtic race to invade Ireland from Greece (around 3200 B.C.), by way of Spain, and identified in their 'Mythological Invasions' with Keasir and her followers.

Entwined Dog border design (1985) originally created as a poster for the music of Michael Law.

18

Book jacket design (1991).

 Fabric design (1992).

Through storm and fire and gloom,
I see it stand
Firm broad and tall,
The Celtic Cross that marks our Fatherland,
Amidst them all!
Druids and Danes and Saxons vainly rage
Around its base;
It standeth shock on shock, and age on age,
Star of our scatter'd race.

Design (1992) suggested by the first verse of
The Celtic Cross, a Scottish poem by Thomas
D'Arcy M'Gee.

Carpet design (1992) adapted from design used
on the picture **Sacred Thread of Life**.

Carpet design (1991) adapted from a page from
the Gospel of St Chad.

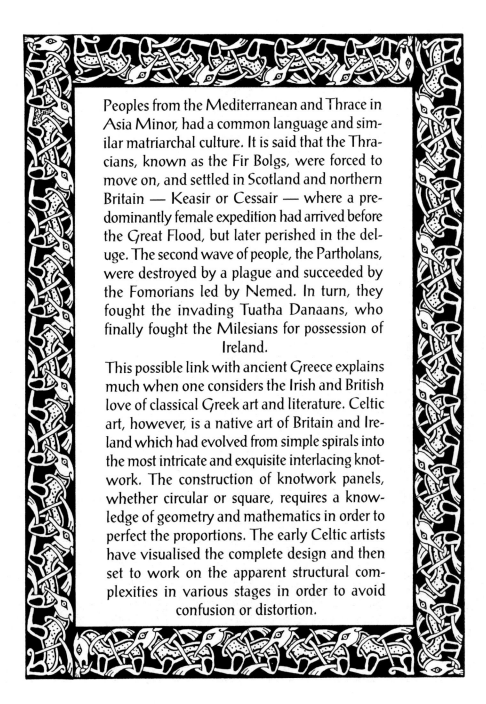

Peoples from the Mediterranean and Thrace in Asia Minor, had a common language and similar matriarchal culture. It is said that the Thracians, known as the Fir Bolgs, were forced to move on, and settled in Scotland and northern Britain — Keasir or Cessair — where a predominantly female expedition had arrived before the Great Flood, but later perished in the deluge. The second wave of people, the Partholans, were destroyed by a plague and succeeded by the Fomorians led by Nemed. In turn, they fought the invading Tuatha Danaans, who finally fought the Milesians for possession of Ireland.

This possible link with ancient Greece explains much when one considers the Irish and British love of classical Greek art and literature. Celtic art, however, is a native art of Britain and Ireland which had evolved from simple spirals into the most intricate and exquisite interlacing knotwork. The construction of knotwork panels, whether circular or square, requires a knowledge of geometry and mathematics in order to perfect the proportions. The early Celtic artists have visualised the complete design and then set to work on the apparent structural complexities in various stages in order to avoid confusion or distortion.

Border design (1991) — a framework of beasts adapted from the **Book of Durrow**.

Scarf panel design (1990).

Celtic wallpaper design (1991) based on the
Lindisfarne Gospels.

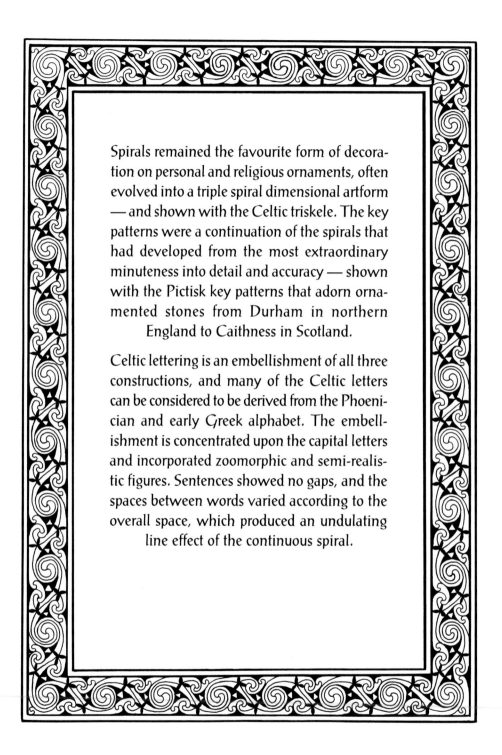

Spirals remained the favourite form of decoration on personal and religious ornaments, often evolved into a triple spiral dimensional artform — and shown with the Celtic triskele. The key patterns were a continuation of the spirals that had developed from the most extraordinary minuteness into detail and accuracy — shown with the Pictisk key patterns that adorn ornamented stones from Durham in northern England to Caithness in Scotland.

Celtic lettering is an embellishment of all three constructions, and many of the Celtic letters can be considered to be derived from the Phoenician and early Greek alphabet. The embellishment is concentrated upon the capital letters and incorporated zoomorphic and semi-realistic figures. Sentences showed no gaps, and the spaces between words varied according to the overall space, which produced an undulating line effect of the continuous spiral.

Spiral border (1985).

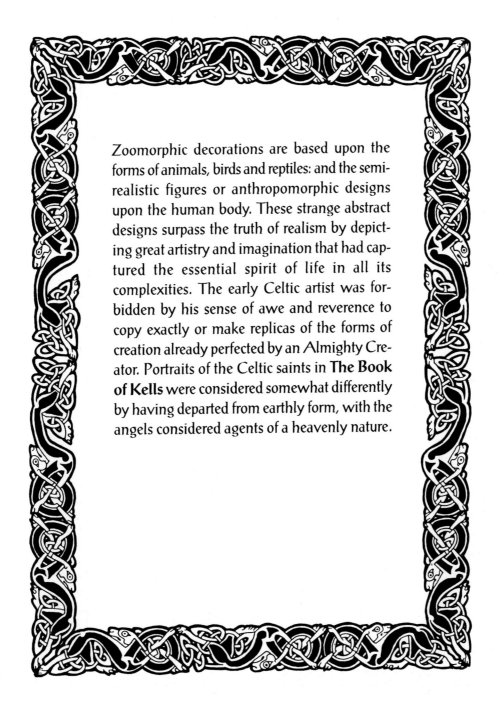

Zoomorphic decorations are based upon the forms of animals, birds and reptiles: and the semi-realistic figures or anthropomorphic designs upon the human body. These strange abstract designs surpass the truth of realism by depicting great artistry and imagination that had captured the essential spirit of life in all its complexities. The early Celtic artist was forbidden by his sense of awe and reverence to copy exactly or make replicas of the forms of creation already perfected by an Almighty Creator. Portraits of the Celtic saints in **The Book of Kells** were considered somewhat differently by having departed from earthly form, with the angels considered agents of a heavenly nature.

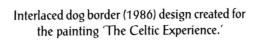

Interlaced dog border (1986) design created for the painting 'The Celtic Experience.'

Carpet design (1992) adapted from various sources.

Discover thou what is
The strong creature from before the flood,
Without flesh, without bone,
Without vein, without blood,
Without head, without feet;
It will neither be older nor younger
Than at the beginning;
For fear of denial,
These are no rude wants
With creatures.

SONG TO THE WIND
Book of Taliesin

©COURTNEY DAVIS 1991

'Prayer for Peace' (1991) with a border originally created in 1984 for **Merlin the Immortal** and later incorporated into a larger work entitled **A Minute's Silence!**

'Tree of Life' (1991) — a design created for use
as a motif on fashion garment.

'Meditation' (1991) — a design produced for
children to colour and used in various workshops
as an aid to concentration and relaxation.

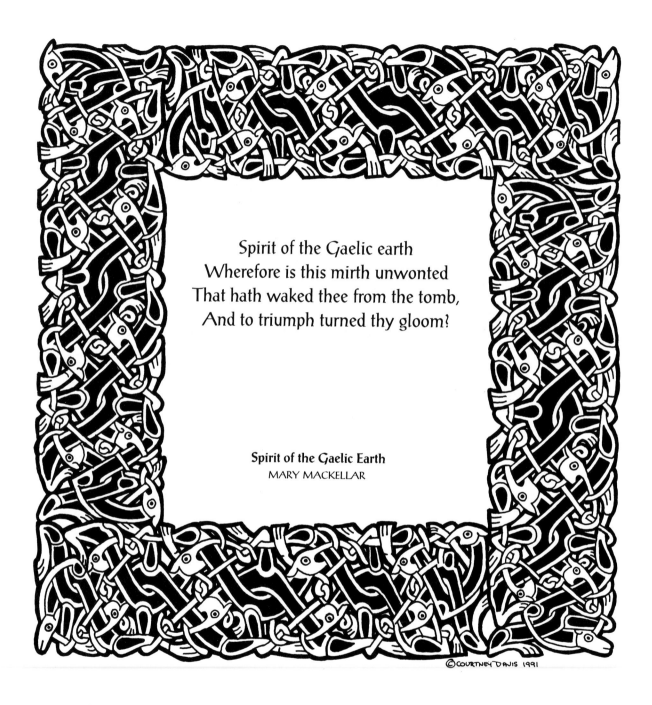

Spirit of the Gaelic earth
Wherefore is this mirth unwonted
That hath waked thee from the tomb,
And to triumph turned thy gloom?

Spirit of the Gaelic Earth
MARY MACKELLAR

©COURTNEY DAVIS 1991

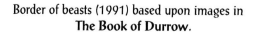

Border of beasts (1991) based upon images in
The Book of Durrow.

'The Energy Spectrum' (1984), with a border design originally used on the cover of **The New Celtic Review** and later used in **Merlin the Immortal**.

Bird motif fabric design (1991).

Book jacket design (1992).

'The Eternal Star' (1992) — a design based
upon the style of Archibald Knox and used as
a motif on fashion garments.

 Fabric design (1992) adapted from the **Lindisfarne Gospels.**

38

Carpet design (1991).

Fabric design (1991).

 St. Patrick (1988).

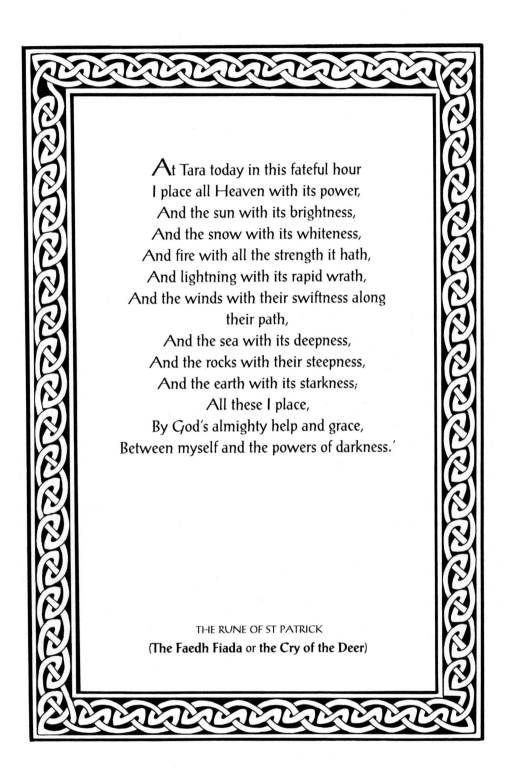

At Tara today in this fateful hour
I place all Heaven with its power,
And the sun with its brightness,
And the snow with its whiteness,
And fire with all the strength it hath,
And lightning with its rapid wrath,
And the winds with their swiftness along
their path,
And the sea with its deepness,
And the rocks with their steepness,
And the earth with its starkness;
All these I place,
By God's almighty help and grace,
Between myself and the powers of darkness.'

THE RUNE OF ST PATRICK

(The Faedh Fiada or the Cry of the Deer)

Simple Celtic border (1992).

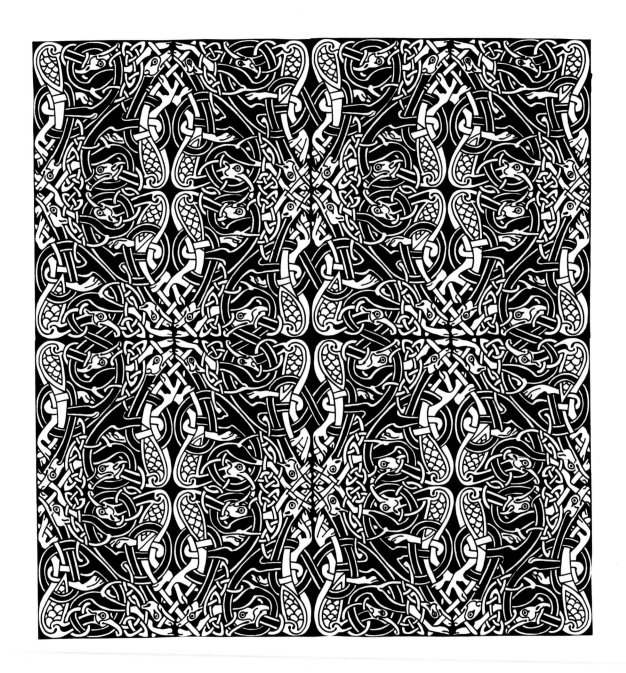

Carpet design (1991).

All circles have an invisible spiralling centre,
The three Druidic 'Circles of Creation'
symbolised the spiritual evolutionary process
designed to unite mankind with Celi — the
Cosmic Creator.

HELENA PATERSON

Original border design for 'The Wasteland'
one of a series of fifteen paintings entitled **The
Symbols of the Grail Quest.**

Fabric design (1992).

Carpet design (1992).

Celtic Mandala (1991) used as a colouring aid
to relaxation.

 Wallpaper or fabric design (1991).

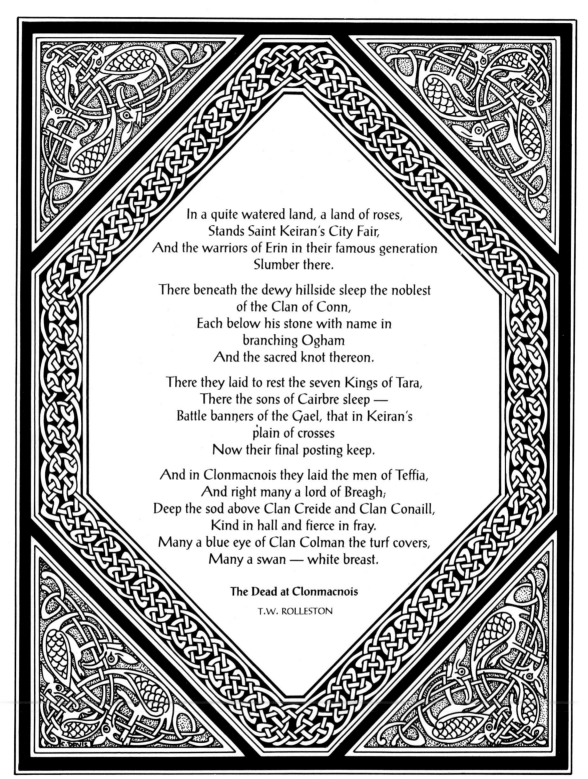

In a quite watered land, a land of roses,
Stands Saint Keiran's City Fair,
And the warriors of Erin in their famous generation
Slumber there.

There beneath the dewy hillside sleep the noblest
of the Clan of Conn,
Each below his stone with name in
branching Ogham
And the sacred knot thereon.

There they laid to rest the seven Kings of Tara,
There the sons of Cairbre sleep —
Battle banners of the Gael, that in Keiran's
plain of crosses
Now their final posting keep.

And in Clonmacnois they laid the men of Teffia,
And right many a lord of Breagh;
Deep the sod above Clan Creide and Clan Conaill,
Kind in hall and fierce in fray.
Many a blue eye of Clan Colman the turf covers,
Many a swan — white breast.

The Dead at Clonmacnois

T.W. ROLLESTON

Celtic mirror design (1990).

 Adapted carpet design from the **Lindisfarne Gospels**.

THE PATH THROUGH
THE LABYRINTH

The Quest for Initiation
into the Western Mystery Tradition

Marian Green

Cover design (1988) originally used as the logo
to The Sacred Dance gallery and shop in
Saffron Walden, Essex, in 1985-86.

Three of eight designs (1988) which were used
as chapter headings in the book **Pathway
Through the Labyrinth**.

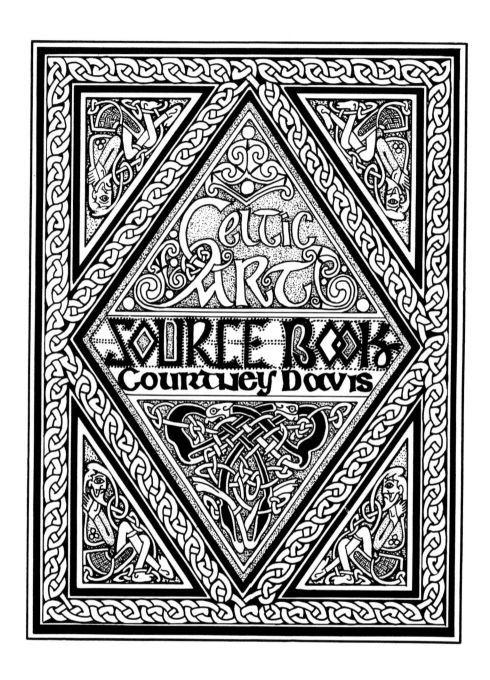

The original cover design for **The Celtic Art Source Book** (1986) which was slightly adapted to emphasise the title.

'The Druids were astronomer-priests who observed numerous stars and planets in our universe besides keeping a close watch on the sun and moon. The rising and setting of the Pleiades constellation was of particular interest in their cosmology; it represented a link with ancestors, ritual death and rebirth of spirit.

Cover design (1992) for the **Symbols of the Grail**. Design created for **The Celtic Art of Courtney Davis** (1984).

Symbols of the
Grail Quest

IAN FORRESTER ROBERTS
ILLUSTRATED BY COURTNEY DAVIS

Title page for **The Symbols of the Grail Quest**
(1991); an adapted design from the Knight of
Cups card in the **Celtic Tarot**.

Title page for **Merlin Awakes** (1989) and adapted from an illustration in **Merlin the Immortal**.

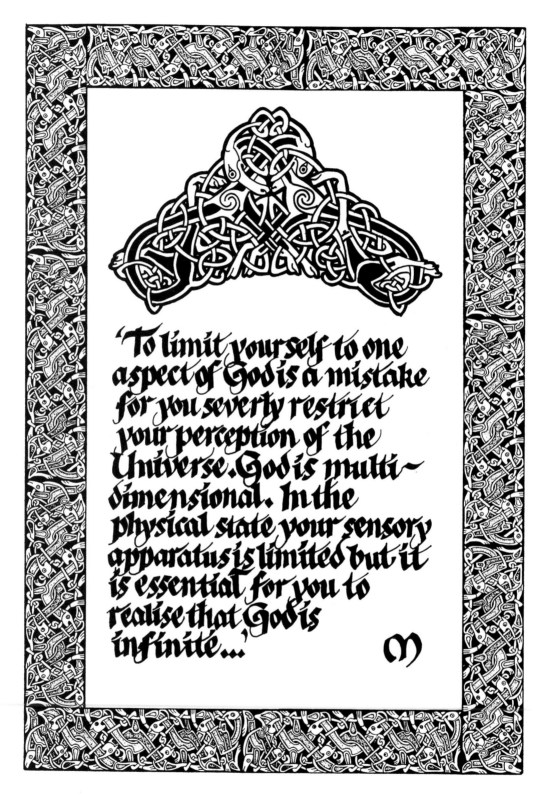

'To limit yourself to one aspect of God is a mistake for you severly restrict your perception of the Universe. God is multi-dimensional. In the physical state your sensory apparatus is limited but it is essential for you to realise that God is infinite...'

'To Limit Yourself' (1989) — an illustration from **Merlin Awakes**. The border is taken from **The Book of Durrow** and added at a later date.

A portrait of Merlin (1984) used to show two aspects of the great seer: on the left the arch-druid receiving the divine light or Awen; on the right the risen Merlin holding in his palm the first of the seven stars of the plough.

The Land Temple (1984) — a design used to depict a pattern of ley lines and sacred sights of Britain. The uppermost point represents York Minster and the lower point the Isle of Wight.

Rhapsody of Hope

The Song of Songs

Karma

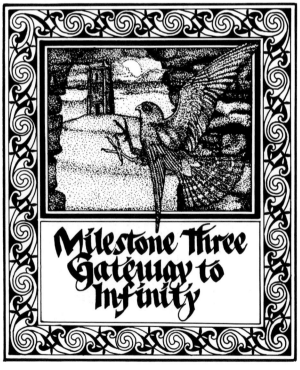

Milestone Three
Gateway to
Infinity

Chapter headings from **Merlin Awakes** (1989).

'Now I a fourfold vision see,
And a fourfold vision is given to
me;
'Tis fourfold in my supreme delight;
And threefold in soft Beulah's night
And twofold always. May God us
keep
From single vision and Newton's
sleep...'

William Blake.

A poem by William Blake as illustrated in a
page from **Merlin Awakes** (1989).

'A Celtic Awakening' (1984), used in books
to portray the awakening of the Celtic Spirit.

COURTNEY DAVIS
ACCOMPANYING BOOK BY
HELENA PATERSON

Working drawing for the cover design of the
Celtic Tarot (1988). A later coloured design
was changed to make the title rather bolder.

'The Hermit' (1987) — a design first produced in black and white as an idea for the direction and overall view of the **Celtic Tarot** pack in general.

'The Wheel of Fortune' (1987) — the second card of the tarot set; first created in black and white.

 'Birds of the Gael' (1980)

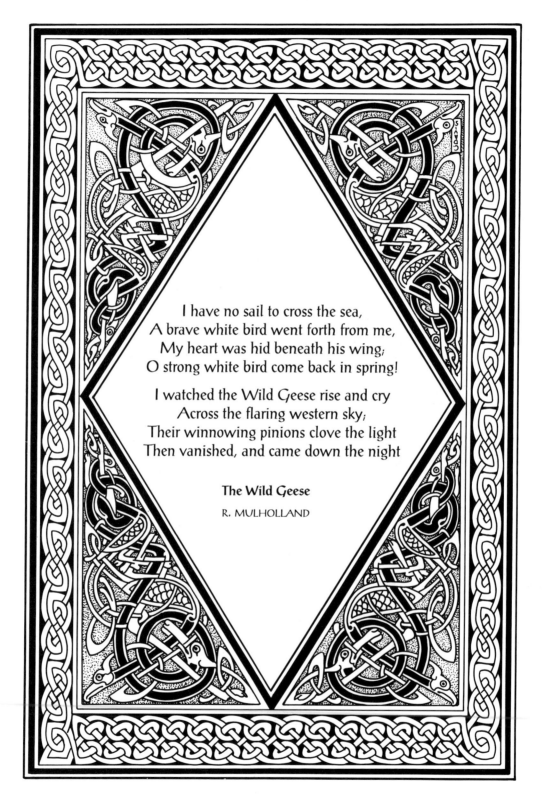

I have no sail to cross the sea,
A brave white bird went forth from me,
My heart was hid beneath his wing;
O strong white bird come back in spring!

I watched the Wild Geese rise and cry
Across the flaring western sky;
Their winnowing pinions clove the light
Then vanished, and came down the night

The Wild Geese

R. MULHOLLAND

Wall hanging design (1989).

The Round Table Zodiac

ILLUSTRATED BY COURTNEY DAVIS · TEXT BY IAN FORRESTER ROBERTS

PUBLISHED BY

Spirit of Celtia ltd.

Book and calendar cover design for **The Round Table Zodiac** (1991) — a series of twelve, images depicting the knights of the table and the zodical signs to which they correspond.

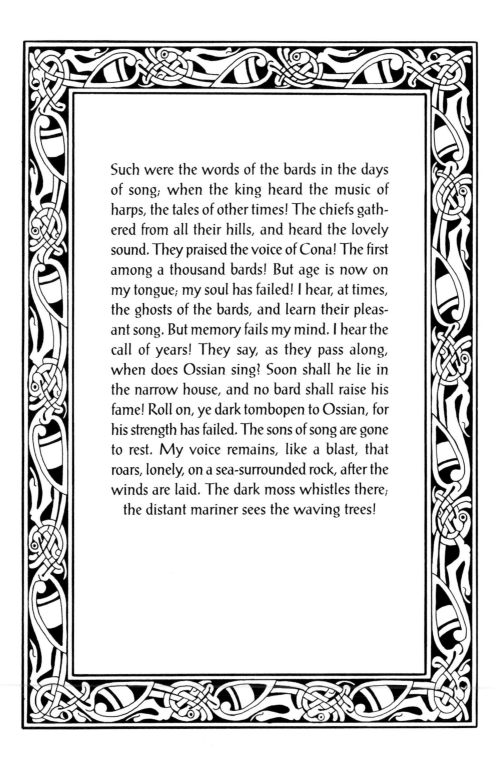

Such were the words of the bards in the days of song; when the king heard the music of harps, the tales of other times! The chiefs gathered from all their hills, and heard the lovely sound. They praised the voice of Cona! The first among a thousand bards! But age is now on my tongue; my soul has failed! I hear, at times, the ghosts of the bards, and learn their pleasant song. But memory fails my mind. I hear the call of years! They say, as they pass along, when does Ossian sing! Soon shall he lie in the narrow house, and no bard shall raise his fame! Roll on, ye dark tombopen to Ossian, for his strength has failed. The sons of song are gone to rest. My voice remains, like a blast, that roars, lonely, on a sea-surrounded rock, after the winds are laid. The dark moss whistles there; the distant mariner sees the waving trees!

Border design (1992) taken from the
Lindisfarne Gospels.

The Seasonal Cycle
Winter
Death - Rebirth · Midnight

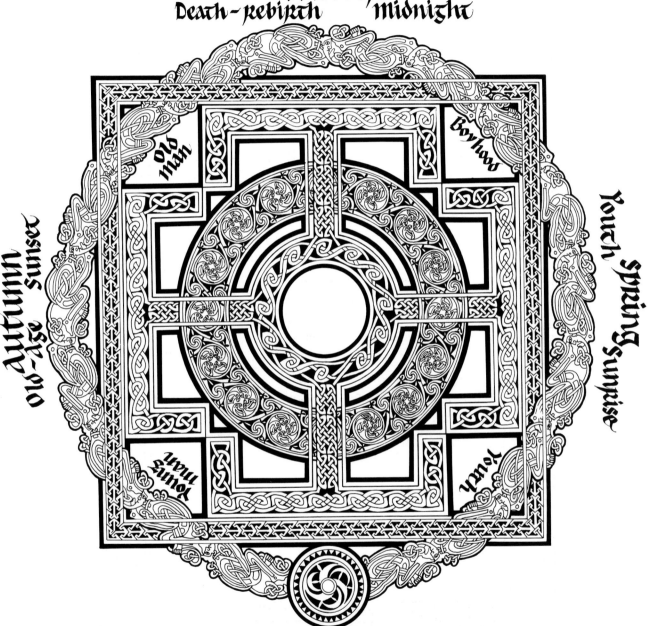

The labels around the design read: Old man · Boyhood · Autumn · Old-Age · Sunset · Youth Spring Sunrise · Young man · Youth

Maturity, Accomplishments · Noon
Summer

'The Seasonal Cycle' (1991) — a poster design
for the Festival of Celtic Spirit at St. James,
Piccadilly, London. Inspiration for the design
was from the Order of Bards, Ovates and
Druids whom are thanked for their permission
for its use.

Business logo design (1991) in the style of
Archibald Knox.

ORIGINAL
CELTIC DESIGNS BY
© COURTNEY DAVIS

Spirit of Celtia logo design (1991) in the style
of Archibald Knox.

A demonstration of Celtic art by Courtney Davis

THE BRITISH LIBRARY
13th DECEMBER 1991 1pm — 4.30pm
AT THE GRENVILLE GALLERY   BRITISH LIBRARY BOOKSHOP
POSTER DESIGNED BY COURTNEY DAVIS FOR SPIRIT OF CELTIA ©

Poster design for the British Library (1991) and
commissioned to coincide with the Library's
'Making of England' Exhibition.

Carpet design (1991) created for the
demonstration at the British Library.

74

 Anglo Saxon pin design (1992) adapted from
one of a triple pin set exhibited at the British
Library Exhibition.

Anglo pin design (1992).

'Merlin the Magician', an original design
(1991) for the **Encyclopedia of Arthurian
Legends** and later used on textiles.

'Gaia' (1991) — an original design for textiles.

Aisling air Dhreach Mna — A Vision of a Fair Woman

Tell us some of the charms of the stars;
Close and well set were her ivory teeth;
White as canna upon the moor
Was her bosom the tartan bright beneath.
Her countenance looked like the gentle buds
Unfolding their beauty in early Spring;
Her yellow locks like gold-browed hills;
And her eyes like the radiance the sunbeams bring.

ANON

Guinevere (1991).

 79

A design for stained glass (1991).

Myrddin — Merlin — as depicted in a design
originally created (1991) for the **Encyclopedia
of Arthurian Legends**.

Merlin, Merlin! where art thou going
So early in the day, with thy black dog!
Oi! Oi! Oi!
I have come here to search the way,
To find the red egg
The red egg of the marine serpent,
By the sea in the hollow of the stone.
I am going to seek in the valley
The green water-cress, and the golden grass,
And the top branch of the oak,
In the wood by the fountain.

ANON

Border design for **Merlin the Immortal** (1984).

© COURTNEY DAVIS 1991

Celtic cross (1991).

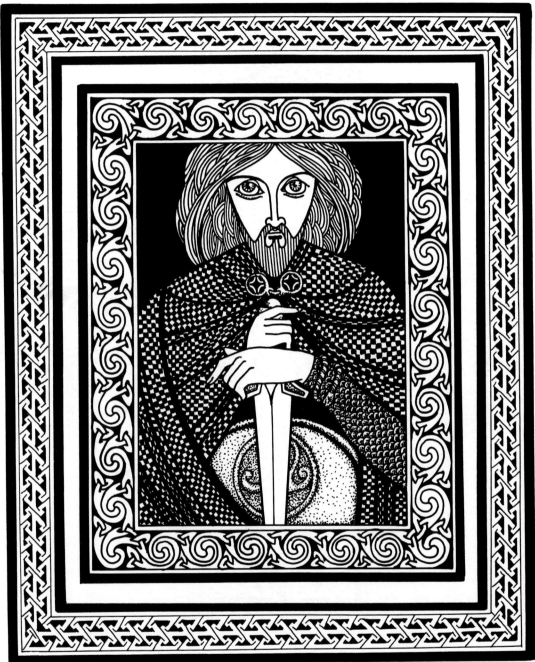

©COURTNEY DAVIS 1991

Design for the **Encyclopedia of Arthurian
Legends** (1991) adapted from the 'King of
Swords' in the **Celtic Tarot**.

'The Glass Isle' (1990) — a cover design
commissioned for the music of Michael Law
entitled **The Glass Isle**.

 'A Knight's Destiny' (1991) — a cover design
for the music of Philip Le Breton.

Celtic magical tradition in Britain and Ireland
(1991) as a cover design for a book by Steve
Blamiries, which also includes four black and
white illustrations.

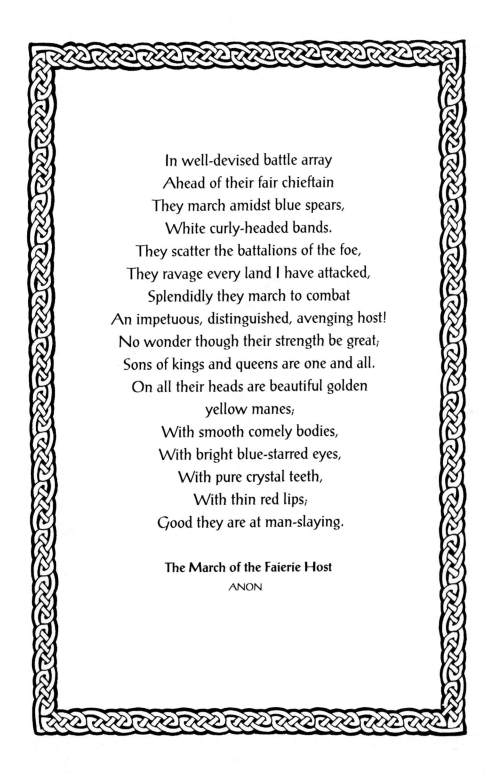

In well-devised battle array
Ahead of their fair chieftain
They march amidst blue spears,
White curly-headed bands.
They scatter the battalions of the foe,
They ravage every land I have attacked,
Splendidly they march to combat
An impetuous, distinguished, avenging host!
No wonder though their strength be great;
Sons of kings and queens are one and all.
On all their heads are beautiful golden
yellow manes;
With smooth comely bodies,
With bright blue-starred eyes,
With pure crystal teeth,
With thin red lips;
Good they are at man-slaying.

The March of the Faierie Host
ANON

Simple Celtic knotwork design (1992).

'The Celtic Experience' (1984).

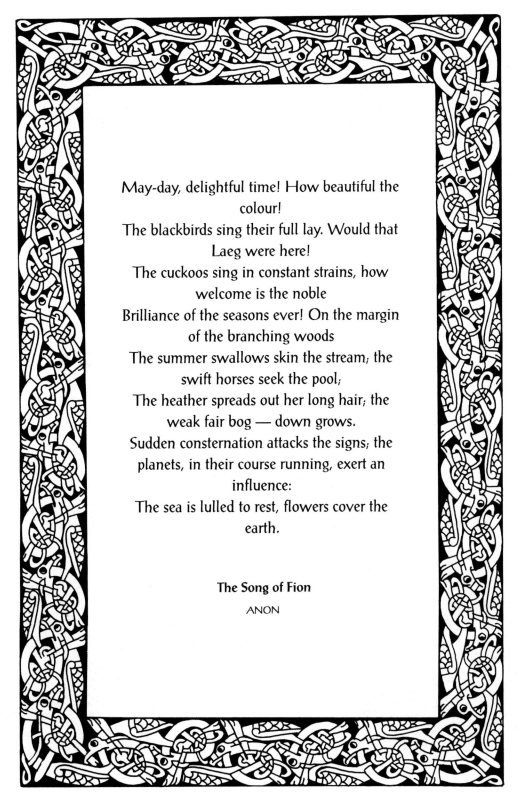

May-day, delightful time! How beautiful the colour!
The blackbirds sing their full lay. Would that Laeg were here!
The cuckoos sing in constant strains, how welcome is the noble
Brilliance of the seasons ever! On the margin of the branching woods
The summer swallows skin the stream; the swift horses seek the pool;
The heather spreads out her long hair; the weak fair bog — down grows.
Sudden consternation attacks the signs; the planets, in their course running, exert an influence:
The sea is lulled to rest, flowers cover the earth.

The Song of Fion
ANON

Celtic bird border design (1991) adapted from one of the pages from the **Gospels of Saint Chad**.

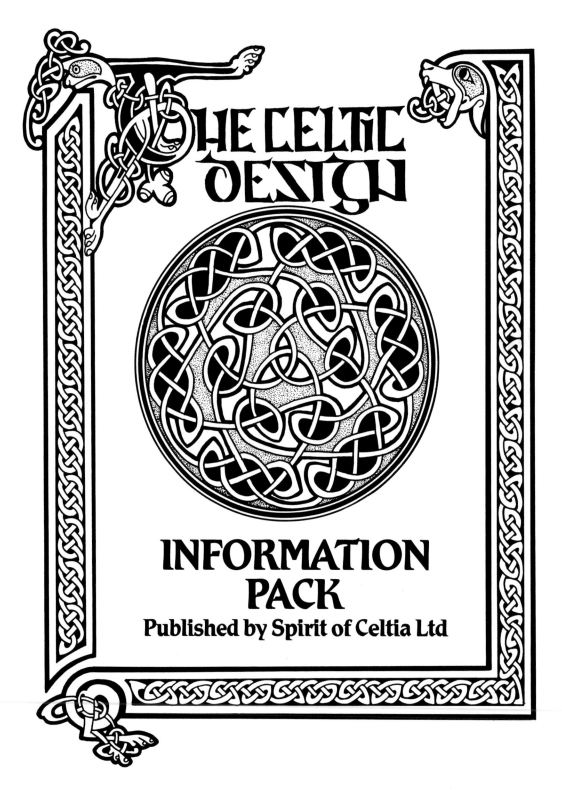

THE CELTIC DESIGN

INFORMATION
PACK

Published by Spirit of Celtia Ltd

Cover design for an information pack (1992).

Till the soil — bid cities rise —

Be strong, O Celt — be rich, be wise —

But still, with those divine grave eyes,

Respect the realm of mysteries.

WILLIAM SHARP

Celtic dog circular design (1991).

'The Celtic Spirit', created originally in 1992 as a poster for an exhibition in 1990 at Ar Bed Kelteik in Brittany and re-drawn and embellished for an article in **Celtic Connection**, February 1992.

acknowledgements

My thanks go out to Dimity whose love and kindness has given me the spirit to work. To Helena Paterson for her inspiration and guidance when my creativity hits a wall, to Chris Roberts for his faith in my work and who aims to set my world in order and finally Stuart Booth who offered me the chance to put these images into a book.

To you who have bought this book may it inspire you as the energy to produce it has inspired me.

May all of your lights shine.

Courtney Davis
Abbotsbury, Dorset 1992

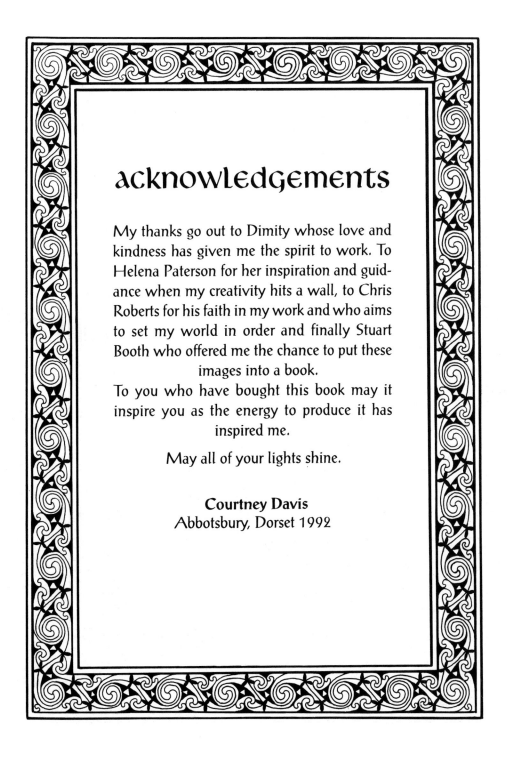

index